Park the car, then we start rhymin'

The only thing we had to free our

VOICES IN HIP-HOP / KENDRICK LAMAR

I made allegi
made a prom
bleeding
You k
still w
Kendr

Published by Creative Education and Creative Paperbacks
P.O. Box 227, Mankato, Minnesota 56002
Creative Education and Creative Paperbacks
are imprints of The Creative Company
www.thecreativecompany.us

Design by Tom Morgan
Art direction by Graham Morgan

Images by Alamy Stock Photo/Jared Milgrim, 22, Scott Hemenway, 16; Getty Images/C Flanigan, 10, Christopher Polk, 37, David Becker, 18–19, Jason Koerner, 44, Johnny Nunez, 40, Moses Robinson/BET, 24, Roger Kisby, 13, Timothy Norris, 9; Instagram/kendricklamar, 46; Wikimedia Commons/Batiste Safont, cover, 4, 43, Fuzheado, 30, Jon Elbaz, 29, Jørund Føreland Pedersen, 3, Kenny Sun, 2, 32–33, Unknown, 15, Zfigueroa, 25

Library of Congress Cataloging-in-Publication Data
Names: Jones, Casey DW, author.
Title: Kendrick Lamar / Casey DW Jones.
Description: Mankato, Minnesota : Creative Education and Creative Paperbacks, 2026. | Series: Voices in hip-hop | Includes index. | Audience: Ages 12–15 | Audience: Grades 7–9 | Summary: "Listen up! It's Kendrick Lamar, the thought-provoking hip-hop artist. Part biography, part song lyric collection, this music-fueled title for high school readers celebrates the rapper's journey and voice. Includes a selected discography and index"– Provided by publisher.
Identifiers: LCCN 2024050280 (print) | LCCN 2024050281 (ebook) | ISBN 9798889892809 (library binding) | ISBN 9781682776469 (paperback) | ISBN 9798889893912 (ebook)
Subjects: LCSH: Lamar, Kendrick, 1987–Juvenile literature. | Rap musicians–United States–Biography–Juvenile literature.
Classification: LCC ML3930.L136 J65 2026 (print) | LCC ML3930.L136 (ebook) | DDC 782.421649092 [B]–dc23/eng/20241023
LC record available at https://lccn.loc.gov/2024050280
LC ebook record available at https://lccn.loc.gov/2024

Printed in India

ance that

ise to see you

reasons but

r know my life

A Compton's

VOICES IN HIP-HOP

KENDRICK LAMAR

CASEY DW JONES

CREATIVE EDUCATION / CREATIVE PAPERBACKS

contents

• • •

Foreword

• • •

"He's amazing, man. Kendrick is one of those artists that we call 'forever artists.' He could disappear for f— five years, or something like that, and come back and f— our heads up, you know? Some artists feel like, 'I have to do something all the time, so I won't be forgotten.' That's not him. He can disappear and come back with something that's shocking, that's amazing, and everybody's gonna tune in and listen."

—DR. DRE, *HART TO HEART*, S3 E3, JULY 13, 2023

Kendrick Lamar performs in San Jose, California, in 2012.

Introduction

Kendrick Lamar has altered the landscape of hip-hop as we know it, and the reach of his impact continues to grow. Fans are drawn to the depth of his storytelling, his heart, and his ability to talk about important issues.

Lamar has never shied away from uncomfortable truths. His lyrics are rooted in his struggles growing up as a young Black man in Compton. He also speaks to the experiences of African Americans everywhere. He challenges societal norms and expectations. He is fearless and honest. This has inspired the next generation of artists to use their own voices to effect change.

Lamar's artistic style is unique and ever evolving. It's not just what he has to say; it's how he says it. His lyrics gain force through his ability to adapt his rapping style. Lamar's delivery is agile. He can bust out rapid-fire rhymes and then seamlessly switch to a slower speed. This flexibility allows him to express many emotions.

Kendrick Lamar is considered one of hip-hop's top artists because of his skill and depth. He captivates his audience. Music writers and other hip-hop artists consider Lamar one of the most influential hip-hop voices of his time. It's no wonder he is the only rap artist to be awarded the Pulitzer Prize for Music.

Growing Up in Compton

• • •

Hot sauce all in our Top Ramen
Park the car, then we start rhymin'
The only thing we had to free our mind
Then freeze that verse when we see dollar signs

—FROM "MONEY TREES" ON THE 2012 ALBUM *GOOD KID, M.A.A.D CITY*

Kendrick Lamar Duckworth was born June 17, 1987, in Compton, California. He is named after singer-songwriter Eddie Kendricks of the Temptations. Kendrick is the first child of Kenneth "Kenny" Duckworth and Paula Oliver, both African Americans from the South Side of Chicago, Illinois. Kenny and Paula relocated to Compton in 1984. Kenny needed to get away from his gang affiliations in Chicago. Kendrick was an only child until age seven. He was eventually joined by two younger brothers and a younger sister.

Kendrick grew up in a low-income environment. Most of the time, he and his family lived in Section 8 housing. At other times, they were houseless. Kendrick was not a member of a gang, but he had friends who ran with the Westside Pirus. Crime and violence were commonplace in the neighborhood. Kendrick witnessed his first murder

Kendrick Lamar, circa 2012

outside his apartment unit when he was five years old. He later became acquainted with police brutality during the 1992 Los Angeles riots.

LA RIOTS

In 1992, four Los Angeles police officers were acquitted (freed of criminal charges) in the beating of a Black man named Rodney King. The incident was recorded on video, so the violence was widely seen across the United States. Shortly after the verdict came in, L.A. became a battleground. Six days of violence, looting, and arson tore the city apart. The primary area affected was South Central L.A. The National Guard was called in to stop the riots. In the end, more than 60 people died, and thousands were injured. There was also significant property damage. This event highlighted the long-standing racial tensions in Los Angeles.

Despite the hardships, Kendrick's family stayed together and stayed strong. During Kendrick's childhood, he didn't receive formal religious instruction, but he was taught the Bible by his grandmother. As an adult, Kendrick would explore his spiritual journey in his lyrics.

Compton sparked Kendrick's interest in hip-hop music. When he was eight years old, he watched the filming of rap artist Tupac Shakur's "California Love" music video while sitting on his father's shoulders. The good and the bad of Compton would strongly inform Kendrick's future in music.

Music was always around Kendrick. His parents threw house parties every Friday. They played everything from oldies and '90s R&B to hip-hop and gangsta rap. During high school, Kendrick performed under the stage name K.Dot and freestyled for his classmates. He formed a friendship with Dave Free, and the pair began recording music together. Kendrick's first mixtape was released in 2003, when he was just 16 years old.

In actuality, it's a trip how we trip off of colors
I wonder if I'll ever discover a passion like you and recover
The life that I knew as a young'un in pajamas and dun-ta-duns

—FROM "SING ABOUT ME, I'M DYING OF THIRST" ON THE 2012 ALBUM *GOOD KID, M.A.A.D CITY*

Book Smarts Meet Street Smarts

• • •

"Everybody that I touched physically, they ended up dead or in jail."

—KENDRICK LAMAR IN A 2014 *SPIN MAGAZINE* ARTICLE

Kendrick Lamar's education occurred outside the school walls just as much as it did inside them. He always possessed a desire for self-improvement, beyond his studies. During his time at Centennial High School, he was a committed student and received high grades. He possessed quick and sharp smarts and a strong will to succeed. He remained focused on being a top student despite the challenges of everyday life in urban Compton—challenges such as his brother doing time in jail.

Kendrick said in a 2014 *Spin Magazine* article, "I remember [my brother] saying, like, he wanted to be the hardest gang member; that's what he wanted to be."

Kendrick's 2012 album *good kid, m.A.A.d city* is filled with stories about growing up in Compton. The track "Backseat Freestyle" features an obsession with the money, power, drugs, and guns that surrounded him. But in the song, he promises to stay true to his vision. "Martin had a dream / Martin had a dream / Kendrick have a dream."

Kendrick's dream of getting out and making something of himself is a frequent theme on the album. On "Sing About Me, I'm Dying of Thirst," he talks about how rapping gave him purpose. Rapping helped Kendrick avoid gang life. It kept him off the streets.

Kendrick was already dropping mixtapes by his senior year of high school. He knew what he wanted to do with his life. And thankfully, he kept a notebook full of rhymes. He had some good friends and mentors who saw he could be a great poet and rapper and gave him support.

Even though he became increasingly focused on becoming a famous rapper, Kendrick remained an avid reader. He wanted to understand human nature. His dedication to broadening his view profoundly shaped his art. It's unlikely he'd be considered one of the best rap artists of all time if he hadn't put so much energy toward his quest for knowledge and understanding.

...Pay attentio
that one
decision
changed bot
of they lives
...One curse at

A Poet Is Born

By the time Kendrick entered middle school, he had already witnessed multiple shootings and murders. These experiences informed his emotional makeup and shaped the things he would grow up to rap about. But Kendrick wouldn't be the artist he is today if not for his seventh-grade poetry teacher, Regis Inge.

Inge immediately saw Kendrick's talent and knew he was a wordsmith in the making. At the time, tensions from a local gang war had seeped into Kendrick's school. Inge looked at poetry as a way to take the edge off. He believed that if his students could unpack their feelings and voice their frustrations, they wouldn't resort to violence. This philosophy was met with resistance, however. The neighborhood boys weren't used to expressing their feelings. So, Inge drew a line from poetry to hip-hop music. He explained how many of the students' idols were rappers, and rappers are poets.

Kendrick took a strong liking to poetry and put everything he had into creative writing. Inge didn't make it easy on him either. He pushed Kendrick to go deeper, to strengthen his vocabulary and understanding of complex issues. Inge's feedback motivated Kendrick to be the best. The budding poet began writing and rapping constantly about what he knew: life on the streets.

Kendrick's best friend from childhood, Matt Jeezy, remembers when Kendrick rapped for 20 minutes straight while walking home from high school one day. Jeezy knew then that all Kendrick had to do was stay alive and stay out of jail, and he would make it. The two friends helped keep each other's focus on school and basketball—and away from the gang lifestyle.

Unfortunately, at age 16, Kendrick started partying, drinking, and hanging out with a rougher crowd. His father didn't want to see his son make the same mistakes he had made in his youth. He stressed that concern to Kendrick, who, thankfully, listened. Inge, Jeezy, and Kendrick's dad, Kenny, all helped motivate and support Kendrick. They had his back, and because of that, he was able to take his art to the next level.

From left, Kendrick Lamar, Jay Rock, Glasses Malone, Detail, ROK, and Kapeash

The Artist Emerges

Kendrick Lamar's raw talent was evident from his early days, but he still needed years of patience and luck to make it big. Many credit his "discovery" and commercial success to Andre Romelle Young—better known as Dr. Dre. However, a lot went down before the young poet crossed paths with the famous pioneer of West Coast gangsta rap.

In 2004, at age 17, Lamar began releasing a series of mixtapes under the name K.Dot. His first mixtape grabbed the attention of Anthony "Top Dawg" Tiffith's Top Dawg Entertainment (TDE), and he signed a contact with the label in 2005. Although Lamar didn't know it at the time, the TDE founder had had multiple encounters on the

streets with Kenny Duckworth, Lamar's father, back in the 1980s. In fact, Tiffith had spared Kenny's life during a robbery. Had Tiffith not done that, Kenny would've died, and his son would've grown up without a father. Lamar raps about this on the 2017 track "DUCKWORTH."

In 2009, Lamar formed the group Black Hippy, which featured rappers Herbert "Ab-Soul" Stevens, Jay Rock, and Quincy "Schoolboy Q" Hanley. That year, he also dropped the alias K.Dot and started rapping under his real name. He wanted his name to reflect his artistic authenticity. Lamar would not release his first full studio album, *Section.80*, until 2011, with TDE. Powered by the hit singles "A.D.H.D." and "HiiPoWeR," the album sold more than 500,000 units and went certified gold.

The success of *Section.80* led to Lamar signing with Warner/Chappell Music before finally landing with Interscope Records and Aftermath Entertainment (the label founded by Dr. Dre) in 2012. Lamar released *good kid, m.A.A.d city* later that year. It sold more than three million copies and was nominated for seven Grammy Awards in 2014.

Lamar's third album, *To Pimp a Butterfly*, debuted in 2015 and sold more than a million copies. Lamar won five Grammy Awards for this effort. In early 2017, he released his fourth studio album, *DAMN.*, which also went triple platinum and won him another five Grammys.

Although it may seem like Lamar burst onto the music scene, his success was the result of years of hard work and dedication. He didn't start selling millions of albums until he was 25 years old, which some consider to be "old" in the rap game.

First Studio Album

• • •

In the 2010s, hip-hop was in a state of flux. Many fans of the genre wanted it to get back to its socially conscious and melodic roots. Lamar helped lead that charge. He offered the public a stark contrast to other popular rappers of the day. To many, his first studio album, *Section.80,* felt like a breath of fresh air when it dropped in 2011.

At the time, Kanye West (now known as Ye) and Jay-Z were at the top of the charts. The genre was overrun by flashiness and mad obsession with money and status. Unclear vocal delivery was widespread, and rap styles could be quite abrasive and unmelodic. Many listeners wanted a return to more grooves, more melody, and more harmony. Some thought hip-hop was at an all-time low.

SECTION

In many ways, *Section.80* was a return to laid-back '90s hip-hop and rap. It's full of groovy beats and soothing, soulful backing vocals. Horns run throughout. And it wasn't just the music that captivated fans; it was also Lamar's message. He refers to his debut single, "Hiiipower," produced by J. Cole, as a "movement" in an interview on *The Come Up Show* (July 1, 2011):

"A lot of people don't understand . . . They think it's just a song. It's really a big movement that we've got in L.A. that's spreading like wildfire. Now, 'Hiiipower': the three i's represent heart, honor, and respect. That's how we carry ourselves in the streets, and just in the world, period. Hiiipower, it basically is the simplest form of representing just being above all the madness, above all the bulls—. No matter what the world is going through, you're always going to keep your self dignity and carry yourself with this manner that it don't phase you. You know what I'm saying? Whatever you think negative is in your life, overcoming that and still having that self-respect."

Section.80 proved to record labels, and to the industry, that there was a market for socially conscious rap. Lamar's next two albums went on to prove, with their commercial success and critical acclaim, that Kendrick Lamar's music was a game changer for the genre and for the industry. He also earned the respect of his peers. He was soon opening concerts for Kanye and Drake.

Every day we fight the system just to make our way
We've been down for too long, but that's all right
We was built to be strong 'cause it's our life, na-na-na
Every day we fight the system (we fight the system, we fight the system)
(Never liked the system)

—FROM "HIIIPOWER" ON THE 2011 ALBUM *SECTION.80*

FIRST STUDIO ALBUM

Kendrick Lamar receives the Pulitzer Prize for Music in 2018.

Black Lives Matter

In 2015, hundreds of Black Lives Matter (BLM) activists assembled at Cleveland State University, in Ohio. It was a time to meet, socialize, and strategize. During the conference, news of Sandra Bland's death arrived. She was a Black woman who was found dead in a jail cell in Texas after a traffic stop. Someone at the conference played "Alright," a song from Lamar's album *To Pimp a Butterfly*. It soon became a Black Lives Matter anthem.

Senseless deaths continued: Alton Sterling, Philando Castile, Stephon Clark... Black Lives Matter reached its height in 2020, in the wake of the murder of George Floyd by Minneapolis, Minnesota, police officers. Protests spread across the globe. Millions of people took to the streets to demand justice and reform in the United States and elsewhere. And Lamar's music was there.

Kendrick Lamar performs on the The DAMN. Tour in Boston, Massachusetts, in 2017.

Because of his social impact, Lamar received the Pulitzer Prize for Music in 2018 for the album *DAMN.* The prestigious award lent legitimacy to hip-hop as a true art form, something that the music genre had been lacking in much of the world outside its immediate community. Lamar is the first, and only, rap artist to have received such an honor.

And we hate po-po
Wanna kill us dead in the street for sure, n—
I'm at the preacher's door
My knees getting' weak and my gun might blow
But we gon' be alright

—FROM "ALRIGHT" ON THE 2015 ALBUM *TO PIMP A BUTTERFLY*

An Emotional Journey

Fame affects people in strange ways—some good, some bad. Lamar's widespread success overwhelmed him at first. He didn't quite feel comfortable with his newfound celebrity status and still didn't feel like he had found his place in the world.

During the recording of his 2015 album *To Pimp a Butterfly,* Lamar struggled with his mental health. He fought depression. He was concerned about his family and friends. They were still enduring a hard life in Compton, while he was enjoying success. In an interview with MTV, Lamar said:

"Psychologically, it messes your brain up. You living *this* life, you know what I'm saying, but you still have to face the realities of *this* . . . I gotta get back off that tour bus and go to these funerals."

To Pimp a Butterfly

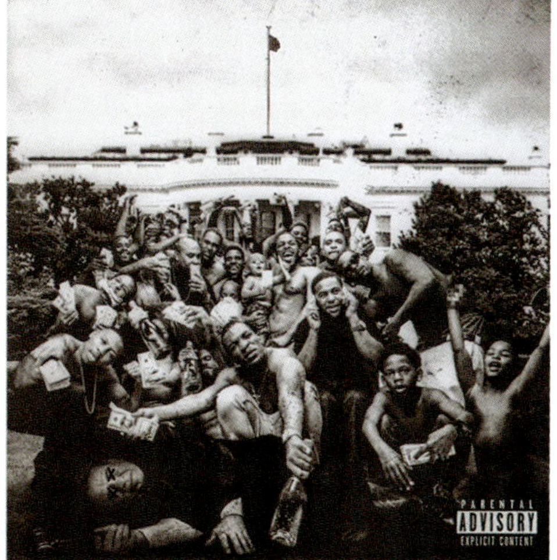

Lamar mentions his struggle with mental health often on the *TPAB* album. And it wasn't just Compton people on his mind. In 2014, right before recording, Lamar traveled to South Africa. During his time there, he visited Robben Island and saw the prison in which Nelson Mandela, the anti-Apartheid civil rights leader, was kept. The experience moved and inspired him. It also shook him.

Lamar began to see that his struggles growing up in Compton were connected to a larger global story. In a 2016 interview with the Recording Academy, he said:

"I felt like I belonged in Africa. I saw all the things that I wasn't taught. Probably one of the hardest things to do is put [together] a concept on how beautiful a place can be and tell a person this while they're still in the ghettos of Compton. I wanted to put that experience in the music."

Lamar's trip to South Africa was a humbling, yet inspiring experience. It changed the course of his career and directly influenced his work. He explored the big themes that would run through the *TPAB* album: staying true to yourself and finding strength in the face of adversity. Lamar was understanding the power of his celebrity—and the cost that came with it.

How clutch are the people that say they love you?
And who pretending?
How tough is your skin when they turn you in?
Do you show forgiveness?

—FROM "MORTAL MAN" ON THE 2015 ALBUM *TO PIMP A BUTTERFLY*

Spiritual Quest

The album *To Pimp a Butterfly* was celebrated for its social consciousness and unique blend of Black music forms. It's heavily infused with notes of jazz, blues, and funk. However, Lamar's most celebrated work to date is undoubtedly *DAMN.*, the album for which he received the 2018 Pulitzer Prize for Music.

Released in 2017, *DAMN.* features many of the same issues and themes Lamar has been known to explore. He raps about inequality and police brutality. He raps about political turmoil, trauma, and gun violence. But a new layer is the idea of a spiritual quest.

Many of the songs on *DAMN.* allude to biblical concepts, such as the seven deadly sins. The album highlights many of Lamar's personal struggles with fame, reflecting on what his life might have been if he had never become famous. "HUMBLE." is one such track—"humble" being the opposite of "pride," which is one of the seven deadly sins. The album even dropped on Good Friday, a day of religious significance for members of the Christian faith.

I'm so f—n sick and tired of the Photoshop
Show me somethin' natural like afro on Richard Pryor

—FROM "HUMBLE." ON THE 2017 ALBUM *DAMN.*

Throughout this landmark album, Lamar battles his own heart and mind. He's proud of his achievements, but he doesn't want to turn cocky and superficial because of them. He wants to stay humble and real. He knows he's less than perfect. In fact, he's just as lost and confused as everybody else.

The final track, "DUCKWORTH," is about an alternate reality. It shows what may have happened if Lamar's father had been killed in the mid-1980s. Throughout the album, listeners are reminded how decisions affect others. Sometimes our fates are bound by the decisions of other people. It's clear Lamar's success inspired a prolonged period of deep personal, spiritual, and artistic introspection. Like the riddle that is life, Lamar asks as many questions in DAMN. as he provides answers.

VOICES IN
HIP-HOP

Speaking Out

Because of his celebrity, Lamar's political journey has been a public one. And sometimes, it's been awkward. He's real in the way he speaks and raps, even if it's not what some people would call "politically correct." Most of his career has been based on fighting the institutions that uphold white supremacy. To Lamar, there is little difference between mass incarceration of Black people and slavery.

It's no shock that a kid from Compton who idolized Tupac Shakur would go on to make art about injustice. (Shakur was raised by members of the Black Panthers, a Black revolutionary party founded in the late 1960s.) Lamar's seven-minute performance at the 2016 Grammys was electric. Viewed by a national audience of about 25 million people, it was a turning point in U.S. discussions about race. Lamar hit the stage dressed in prison garb and chains and then launched into an intense, unflinching performance of "The Blacker the Berry" and "Alright," from his *To Pimp a Butterfly* album. The rapid-fire lyrics, strobe lights, drumbeats, and simulated gunshots

demanded attention. Many activists believe that *TPAB* is an ode to the Black Lives Matter movement. With lyrics like these from "The Blacker the Berry," it's not hard to see why: "My hair is nappy, my d— is big, my nose is round and wide / You hate me, don't you? / You hate my people, your plan is to terminate my culture."

In another political area, Lamar showed support for fellow recording artist Frank Ocean in an open letter following Ocean's coming out as gay in 2012. He did so even though the hip-hop community was known for discriminating against queer people. However, Lamar has also been criticized for the way he speaks about transgender people in the song "Auntie Diaries," released in 2022. He misgenders them and uses anti-LGBTQ+ slurs throughout the track. Some say that Lamar is simply highlighting his past ignorance and have praised him for being real about his evolution on the issue.

I'm the biggest hypocrite of 2015
Once I finish this, witnesses will convey just what I mean
I mean, it's evident that I'm irrelevant to society
That's what you're telling me, penitentiary would only hire me
Curse me till I'm dead

—FROM "THE BLACKER THE BERRY" ON THE 2015 ALBUM *TO PIMP A BUTTERFLY*

Kendrick Lamar accepts a Best Rap Album Grammy in 2023.

Personal Life

The cat is out the bag, I am not your savior
I find it just as difficult to love thy neighbors
Especially when people got ambiguous favors

—FROM "SAVIOR" ON THE 2022 ALBUM *MR. MORALE & THE BIG STEPPERS*

onnecting with Dr. Dre was the key moment in Lamar's rap career. It almost didn't happen. Lamar told radio host Howard Stern, "We was eating at Chili's, and we got a call, like, 'Yo, Dr. Dre likes your music.' And we're just like, 'Who the f— is this on the phone? Get out of here' . . . We hung up." Then another call came, and another, and another, and Lamar finally believed Dr. Dre was interested in him.

Dr. Dre did more than just sign Lamar to his record label. He also had a huge impact on Lamar's personal life. He took him under his wing and became a mentor to the

... I picked you up when you fell and cut your knee

... Told you not to cry and

rising star. He helped Lamar keep a level head while navigating the ups and downs of touring and the recording industry.

The other central figure in Lamar's personal life is his high-school sweetheart and fiancée, Whitney Alford. Their shared triumphs and struggles are referenced by Lamar across all of his albums. From long before the couple got engaged in 2015 to now, Lamar has never hesitated to address their issues head-on in his work.

Outside of his art, Lamar keeps his personal life private. Most of the world didn't even know he and Whitney had had their second child until the family of four appeared on the cover art of Lamar's 2022 album, *Mr. Morale & the Big Steppers*. In the image, Lamar is holding his then-three-year-old daughter, Uzi. Whitney stands in the background holding the couple's newborn son, Enoch. In the opening to the album, listeners can hear Whitney say, "Tell them the truth."

Lamar credits Whitney and his children with helping him grow as a person. He views the *Mr. Morale* album as an emotional roadmap to understanding life as the children grow and age into adults.

I picked you up when you fell and cut your knee
Told you not to cry and held you close to me
I hope I'm not too late to set my demons straight
I know I made you wait, but how much can you take?

—FROM "DIE HARD" ON THE 2022 ALBUM *MR. MORALE & THE BIG STEPPERS*

Kendrick Lamar performs in Miami Gardens, Florida, in 2022.

What's Next?

• • •

The album *Mr. Morale & the Big Steppers* dropped in 2022. It was Lamar's fifth studio album and his final project with Top Dawg Entertainment. Lamar executive-produced the album himself, under the pseudonym Oklama.

Like much of his other work, Lamar's *Mr. Morale* is extremely introspective. The album includes experiences and reflections from his therapy journey. He raps around the personal themes of trauma, infidelity, and coping with his celebrity status.

Mr. Morale won Best Rap Album at the 65th Annual Grammy Awards, having received eight nominations. That was the fourth time Lamar had been nominated for Album of the Year. He toured Europe, North America, and Oceania in support of the album. Reviews were positive but also somewhat mixed, with some praising the album's humility and others wanting more of the vibe that *DAMN.* had. In a May 17, 2022, review, *Vulture* music

Mr. Morale & the Big Steppers cover photo

critic Craig Jenkins said, "K.Dot peaced on us, got himself a therapist, and came back to share what he learned, to redraw some boundaries, and to refuse the titles of Voice of a Generation and Best Rapper Alive. His new album, *Mr. Morale & the Big Steppers*, delivers this news with an air of apology. He knows it's not the message people want; he feels it's the one they need."

Despite not wanting to be put on a pedestal, Lamar's relevance in the hip-hop world remains strong. He is still front and center in the American cultural conversation. He was selected to perform at the 2025 Apple Music Super Bowl LIX (59) Halftime Show. In 2025, he won five Grammys for his single "Not Like Us." But will there be a new album? Or will he hang up the mic? On the *Mr. Morale* track "Mirror," Lamar seems to consider it. "Maybe it's time to break it off / Run away from the culture to follow my heart."

People close to Lamar say he's been working on a new album ever since the last one came out. Chances are good that if this is true, his work will spark more hard conversations. Considering how many directions Kendrick Lamar's career has already taken, it's difficult to say which way his art will turn next.

I hope I'm not too late to set my demons straight
I know I made you wait, but how much can you take?

—FROM "DIE HARD" ON THE 2022 ALBUM *MR. MORALE & THE BIG STEPPERS*

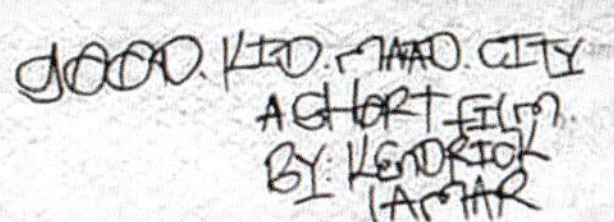

SELECTED WORKS BY KENDRICK LAMAR

EPS

Kendrick Lamar, 2009

MISC.

untitled unmastered., 2016

"Not Like Us," 2024

MIXTAPES

Overly Dedicated, 2010

C4, 2009

No Sleep Til NYC, 2007

Training Day, 2007

Y.H.N.I.C. (Hub City Threat: Minor of the Year), 2004

SOUNDTRACKS

Black Panther, 2018

STUDIO ALBUMS

GNX, 2024

Mr. Morale & the Big Steppers, 2022

DAMN., 2017

To Pimp a Butterfly, 2015

good kid, m.A.A.d city, 2012

Section.80, 2011

INDEX